MW00974872

THANK YOU
MIND

Understanding My Big
Feelings on Tricky Days

Jennifer Cohen Harper

Illustrated by Karen Gilmour

Thank You Mind
Copyright © 2020 Jennifer Cohen Harper

Published by:
PESI Publishing & Media
PESI, Inc.
3839 White Ave.
Eau Claire, WI 54703

Illustrations: Karen Gilmour
Cover: Karen Gilmour & Amy Rubenzer
ISBN: 9781683733454

Library of Congress Cataloging-in-Publication Data

Names: Cohen Harper, Jennifer, author. | Gilmour, Karen, illustrator.

Title: Thank you mind : understanding my big feelings on tricky days /
    Jennifer Cohen Harper ; illustrated by Karen Gilmour.

Description: Eau Claire : PESI Publishing & Media, 2020.

Audience: Ages 4-10

Summary: "This book teaches children how to use mindfulness to
    cope with big feelings and tricky days by noticing their emotions
    without judging them and using self-soothing techniques. It also has a
    note to caregivers at the back of the text to help them assist the child
    in further learning about mindfulness and how they can check in with
    their emotions"-- Provided by publisher.

Identifiers: LCCN 2020027948 | ISBN 9781683733454 (hardcover)

Subjects: Mindfulness (Psychology)--Juvenile literature. | Emotions
    in children--Juvenile literature.

All rights reserved
Printed in Canada

PESI
Publishing
& Media
pesipublishing.com

For every child who ever thought they should make their feelings smaller.
And every grown-up still working to become friends with themselves. — JCH

To Maggie—whose imagination is with me every step of the way. — KG

Welcome Letter

Your mind, like mine, is a thought-making machine, and it has a lot to say! We all have an inner voice that can be like a cheerleader, a coach, or a good friend. But sometimes, that voice can say things that are upsetting or untrue, and that voice can sound more like a critic.

Often our minds are the most chatty when we are experiencing big emotions. In those times, our inner voice can help us understand how we are feeling and encourage us to meet our needs, or it can discourage us and make us feel badly about ourselves.

The good news is that by practicing speaking kindly to ourselves, and noticing the good in the world, we can help our mind learn how to support us. And then, it can be our greatest friend on our tricky days.

Much love,

Jenn

I like my mind and it likes me.

We've figured out a way to be.

My mind is helpful in many ways.

We work hard to help each other on most days.

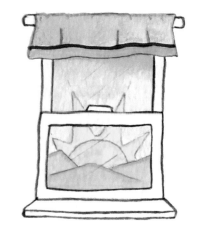

Thank you mind for giving me a pep talk when I need to see that my power never went away.

And I can find it, even on a tricky day.

The world gets confusing.
There's so much to know.

I feel overwhelmed and
don't know where to go.

Then I remember
that I can slow down,
do one thing at a time,
feel my feet on the ground.

There are times when something is coming that's great, and I feel like I'll burst just trying to wait.

But if I listen close, there's a voice that will say,

Looking forward to fun can be part of the play.

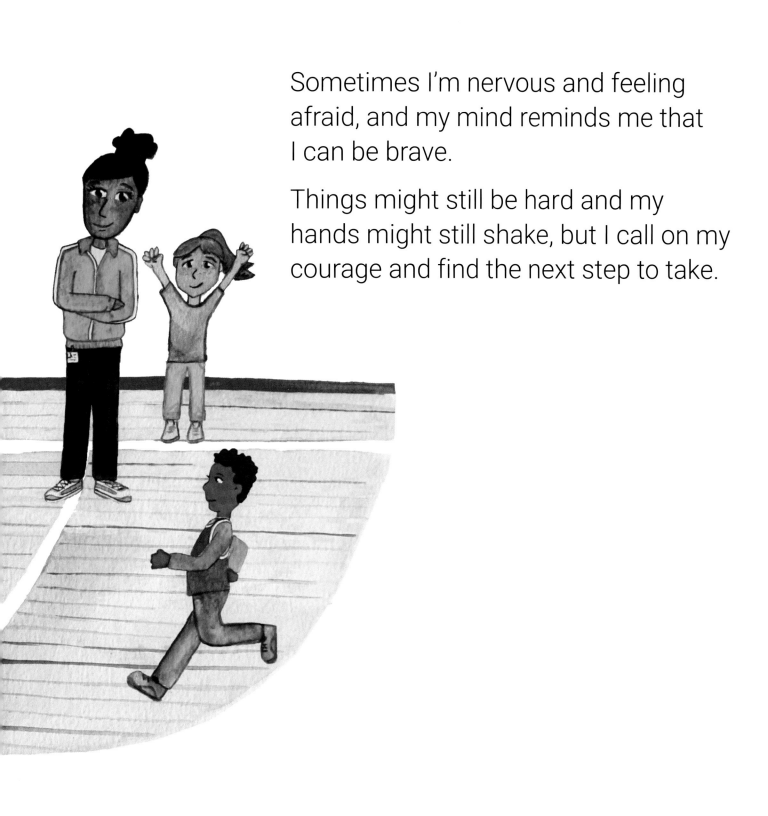

Sometimes I'm nervous and feeling afraid, and my mind reminds me that I can be brave.

Things might still be hard and my hands might still shake, but I call on my courage and find the next step to take.

Sometimes anger fills me up inside, with thoughts and feelings I'd rather hide.

It's hard not to shout, or fight, or cry, but I try to stand tall, say what I need and why.

Excitement can make me want to run
as fast as I can toward what is fun.

But while I'm running,
my mind tells me,

Pay attention.

Enjoy.

*Don't rush past
what you see.*

Life is so filled with things to explore, and each bit that I learn makes me want to learn more.

My mind's like a magnet that pulls thoughts to me, and with each new idea there's a whole world I can see.

Then there are days when the world is so sad,
and it seems like every direction is bad.

My heart feels so heavy, it gets hard to breathe.

Then my mind sends a whisper,
It's ok to grieve.

I notice that others are struggling too, and I don't always know just what I should do.

But things hurt less with a friend close by, so even if it feels tricky, that's what I'll try.

There are times when my friends' lives seem better than mine, and it's hard to find my moment to shine.

But I feel a bit better when I remember what's true: who I am matters more than how well I do.

Sometimes I'm bored
and can't figure out
what to do with myself,
what this day's all about.

It feels like I have nothing
but time and space,
but imagination and creation
can fill up this place!

The joy that I feel when there's love all around
reminds me that peace can often be found
in the tiny moments that make up my day.

My heart and my mind both find rest in the play.

It's not always easy
to find a way through
the tricky and sticky
and messy and new.

Sometimes my mind
is confused and upset
and tells me things
that I'd like to forget.

On those days I try
to breathe out
and breathe in.

Settling my body
is a good place to begin,
reminding myself that
those unhelpful ideas
are often not true.

They grow from my fears.

I don't have to believe
all the thoughts in
my mind, especially
the ones that are
very unkind.

I send some love
to myself and I say,
*Remember your power,
you can find a way.*

Then the part of me that is steady and strong,
the part that knows just where I belong,
comes to give me a hand so I can find
the most helpful and loving ideas in my mind.

The wonders I see in
the sky and the sea,
I know the same magic
lives inside of me.

When I'm amazed by the
world, in awe of the view,
my mind says,
Remember,
you're part of this too.

Checking In With My Feelings Practice

We all experience many emotions every day, and each one of them is an important part of who we are. Take a moment to look at the faces on the other page and consider how you're feeling right now. You can sit or stand, whatever feels steadier and more comfortable.

Put one hand on your heart and one on your belly. Take a few slow, steady breaths, and then ask yourself, *What emotions am I feeling right now?* If nothing comes to mind right away, that's ok! It can take a little while, so try to stay with it and maybe even ask the question again, *How am I feeling right now?*

You may notice that you are feeling more than one emotion, and this is perfectly normal. Sometimes you may feel two things at once, like lonely and angry, or embarrassed and frustrated.

You may even feel two things that seem very different, like sad and happy, or nervous and excited, at the same time. At other times it may be just one feeling that you notice showing up. Try not to worry right now about what is causing your feelings—this activity is about just noticing them.

Once you notice how you are feeling, you may be able to notice that your body responds to your feelings. For example, sometimes we tighten our fists when we are angry, or our belly gets butterflies when we are nervous, or our eyes water when we are sad. Do you notice your body responding to your feelings today? If you do, what do you notice?

Note to Caregivers

Thank you for supporting children and working to help them better understand their own complex human experience.

The inner voice of our minds can be a loving source of support, but for many of our kids (and ourselves!) it is often a source of judgment, criticism, and sometimes unnecessary fearmongering.

Our brains have a negativity bias, designed to help keep us safe. In order to help us learn from negative experiences, our brains register those experiences quickly and hold on to the memories of them strongly. Since learning from positive experiences isn't as critical to survival, the brain doesn't work quite as hard to register or remember them.

Psychologist Rick Hanson describes the human brain as Velcro for negative experiences and Teflon for positive ones. This means it is easier to see the downside than the upside in many situations, especially when big feelings are involved. Even when positive feelings are involved! Have you ever been right in the middle of something good happening, only to find yourself thinking about how bad it will be when it's over? That is the negativity bias at work.

But there is something we can do about it. We can, through self-compassionate and empowering practice, train our brains to be less attuned to the negative, to be more capable of noticing and embracing the positive, and to be better able to learn and grow from challenges.

Childhood is filled with intense emotions. And it should be. Our big feelings are a big part of what makes us human. But when we are overwhelmed by tricky emotions, the negativity bias often kicks in, and instead of welcoming our feelings and learning more about ourselves from them, we try to push them away or become reactive. On the flip side, when we have big positive emotions, it is easy to get so overstimulated that we largely miss savoring the experience.

I hope that in reading this book together with your children, you will use it as an opportunity to talk about their emotions and experiences. By exploring how our minds can support us on tricky days (through self-talk, acceptance, reframing, noticing different perspectives, and savoring the good stuff), we can practice these skills and build a loving relationship with our own minds, learning what it means to truly befriend ourselves.

With love and gratitude,

Jenn

Author & Illustrator

Jennifer Cohen Harper is an educator, author, public speaker, and mother, who works to support all children and teens in the development of strong inner resources through the tools of yoga and mindfulness. Her goal is to help kids, and those who care for them, thrive in the world regardless of their circumstances and navigate the many challenges they face with a sense of personal power and self-awareness. Jenn is the founder and CEO of Little Flower Yoga + Mindfulness. She is the author of *Thank You Body, Thank You Heart* and a wide range of yoga and mindfulness resources for families and educators.

Karen Gilmour has been drawing, painting, coloring, and creating for as long as she can remember. Her art has been seen in books, on back-to-school supplies, and on the walls of classrooms and kids' rooms. When Karen isn't creating art, she is busy as the director of Alluem Kids, an ever-growing yoga program for kids, teens, and families at Alluem Yoga in Cranford, NJ. You can see more of Karen's work by visiting: www.karengilmour.com